IRISH BUS PHOTOGRAPHERS

IRISH BUSES IN THE MID-1960s
A RETURN JOURNEY

Richard Newman

COLOURPOINT BOOKS

Published 2018 by Colourpoint Books
An imprint of Colourpoint Creative Ltd
Colourpoint House, Jubilee Business Park
Jubilee Road, Newtownards, BT23 4YH
Tel: 028 9182 6339
Fax: 028 9182 1900
E-mail: sales@colourpoint.co.uk
Web: www.colourpoint.co.uk

First Edition
First Impression

Designed by April Sky Design, Newtownards
Tel: 028 9182 7195 • Web: www.aprilsky.co.uk

Printed by GPS Colour Graphics Ltd, Belfast

ISBN 978-1-78073-177-3

Front cover: CIÉ Leyland Royal Tiger U52, part of the batch of 38 similar vehicles built in 1954, is seen by Store Street Bus Station (later Busáras)
on 30 June 1965, en route from the city's docklands to the city centre. The batch had 45-seat, rear entrance bodies when new, but were
rebuilt with a front entrance and centre exit when transferred from the provincial fleet to the Dublin City Services fleet.

Rear cover: Two turning circles for short workings were provided on Belfast's Shore Road trolleybus route. One of these was at Fortwilliam, near a former
tram depot. Trolleybuses terminating here displayed route number 8 and Guy BTX 172 is seen on the square setts on 28 July 1965.

CONTENTS

INTRODUCTION

Ironically, it was an enquiry for travel from Belfast Airport to Omagh, while I was working at Portsmouth Enquiry Office, that formulated the decision to take another, more ambitious Irish holiday. The 'indispensable' abc Rail Guide, which I was always reluctant to use, was less than helpful, giving only two daily Belfast to Omagh bus departures – both too early for the lady enquirer who probably thought the town was still rail-served. Of course, no Ulsterbus bus timetables were held. I decided I needed to know more of the Irish transport system.

On Friday 7 July 1967, at 3.00pm, I bade farewell to my Enquiry Office and Telephone Bureau colleagues at Portsmouth, following a three-month secondment there as part of my railway studentship training programme. After a dash home to swallow a meal and gather my luggage, within two-and-a-half hours I was at Havant to join the Portsmouth–Waterloo electric, formed of comfortable, pre-war 'Nelson' 4-COR stock, at the start of my second Irish holiday. This meant I even missed the end of Southern Region steam on the Bournemouth line. My first Irish holiday, confined to Belfast and Dublin, had been in July 1965 (see *Irish Buses in the mid-1960s*, Colourpoint Books, 2007).

At Waterloo, I met with George Wheeler, a colleague from schooldays, who had also joined BR so we both now had the benefit of free passes and privilege travel. We headed to Euston for the 20:40 sleeper to Stranraer Harbour on which berths had been booked, but stops at many West Coast Main Line stations made sleep spasmodic. Since the closure of the direct 'Port Road' line between Dumfries and Stranraer, the sleeper now ran via Kilmarnock and Ayr so it was daylight by the time we reached the Scottish port where *Caledonian Princess* was preparing to sail for Larne at 07:00. Breakfast was taken on the crossing and upon arrival at Larne we joined the multi-purpose diesel (MPD) unit for the journey to Belfast (York Road). Although the trolleybuses were visible outside the station, we were heading for Londonderry so joined a Class 70 diesel-electric set that was still being prepared. Steam was still visible at York Road shed and the ex-Sligo, Leitrim and Northern Counties Railway 0-6-4T *Lough Erne* (a mere 16-years-old) was station pilot.

We broke our journey at Coleraine, changing for Portrush, which still possessed the substantial station building, two signal boxes and a fine collection of lower quadrant signals on wooden posts as the branch was regularly served by steam-hauled excursion trains. I had visited Portrush in 1965, but Coastal Bus Services had taken on work from the Ulster Transport Authority (UTA) in 1966 and operated from a small depot in Dunluce Avenue with a fleet of Leyland Royal Tigers. Examples from Red & White, Ribble, Sunderland District and Yorkshire Traction were in evidence, but the ex-Southdown Duple Elizabethan-bodied coaches familiar to me were out on tour. After lunching in Portrush, we continued to Londonderry, changing again at Coleraine where plenty of UTA Leyland half-cab double-deckers were in evidence. The Portrush branch part of the journey was behind a 'Jeep' 2-6-4T on an excursion train.

Early morning at Stranraer Harbour on Saturday, 8 July 1967 and *Caledonian Princess* awaits departure for Larne on the short sea crossing. This view well illustrates the most convenient rail/ship connections afforded at this port. Shipping services were withdrawn at Stranraer after 20 November 2011, when Stena Line moved its operations to a new facility further north on Loch Ryan.

The MPD unit working Belfast to Londonderry Waterside was strengthened by a single carriage of semi-open stock, which seemed quite elderly (the number 50 sticks in my mind) so we joined it, but it rode so roughly at speed that we moved forward to the main part of the train at Limavady Junction! We arrived at Waterside (the old stone Belfast & Northern Counties Railway station for which a revival is now planned) and made our way over the Craigavon Bridge, passing the County Donegal Railways (CDR) station at Victoria Road and the Great Northern Railway (GNR) one at Foyle Road, both closed, to find our accommodation at Johnny Quigley's Hotel and Bar in Foyle Street, near the yard of James H Bond, manure merchant! I think it would be true to say that Derry City was not yet geared up to tourism in 1967 and Foyle Street was fairly grim – dark and foreboding with several beggars trying their luck. The shabby hotel room, with a view of the

city wall, possessed a mantelpiece with a selection of light switches and fittings as ornamentation. Having settled in, we walked the city walls and noted the Ulsterbus bus presence, including ex-Edinburgh Corporation Tiger Cubs and No 8858, the lengthened Leyland PS2, painted in the new blue and ivory livery. The Londonderry and Lough Swilly Railway Company's ex-demonstrator Leyland Atlantean, No 87, was also observed and photographed.

The following day was a Sunday so travel options were limited. After a good breakfast, we headed along Strand Road, observing one of the Swilly's ex-Southdown Leyland Royal Tiger coaches outside the Great James Street office, well-loaded for a day excursion. We probably passed the wall of the LLSR's Graving Dock station, although we did not know it at the time, en route to Pennyburn where the railway's headquarters until 1953 now served as the main bus depot

Grounded coach bodies in use as stores at the Londonderry and Lough Swilly Railway Company's premises at Pennyburn. It's sad that none of the coach bodies here were saved for the Belfast Transport Museum, sadder still that the company itself folded at Easter 2014.

Sunday 9 July saw us at Strabane where we were able to view some of the remaining County Donegal Railways stock which had been bought by a rich American dentist, Dr Ralph Cox, with a view to shipping it across the Atlantic. The locomotives were *Drumboe* and *Meenglass*.

and works. Various withdrawn half-cab saloons were parked around the yard while the active fleet included all-Leyland PD2s, PS2s and Royal Tigers, including a Saro-bodied example bought new. The former engine shed continued as a workshop while four grounded carriage bodies were in use as stores. No 18 had been a six-wheeler with Cleminson design axles while B11 had been constructed as a bogie coach by RY Pickering for the Londonderry and Burtonport Extension early in the twentieth century. Sadly, these gems would be burned and the opportunity to fill a gap in the Cultra transport collection lost forever. We received a friendly welcome from the Swilly staff and one of the drivers suggested we should visit Letterkenny where a CDR engine (I understand this was *Erne*) still existed, but his colleague commented, "By jabbers, no, you won't get a bus there on a Sunday!" It was decided we should head for

Strabane where two CDR engines and about a dozen carriages survived awaiting collection by a rich American doctor (although they were never to reach the USA). We headed back to the city and joined an Ulsterbus AEC Reliance for Strabane.

The author at Strabane on the trackbed of the Great Northern Railway's 'Derry Road', which the Ulster Transport Authority had closed in 1965. The line from Strabane, in Northern Ireland, reached Londonderry, also in Northern Ireland, by way of the Republic of Ireland. That meant the staff at intermediate stations worked for CIÉ even though their stations rarely, if ever, saw a CIÉ train!

As we arrived, several busloads of residents were heading off for a day's excursion on red and cream CDR Leyland Tiger Cubs new to East Midland. The town seemed fairly deserted, but we found the joint Great Northern and County Donegal stations and the collection of narrow-gauge rolling stock. Track removal on the Great Northern's 'Derry Road' was almost complete, but a signal still stood forlornly and the vandalised ticket office contained timetables and accountancy documents scattered randomly over the floor and a CDR collected return ticket. There was still some time before the bus back to Derry so we enquired at The County Tyrone Dining Rooms – situated in a front parlour – whether food was being served. The gentleman of the house summoned Moira, his elderly wife, from the kitchen and we were provided with cream crackers although another man was heartily devouring a full Sunday roast.

On the Monday morning (10 July), we departed Quigley's and headed round to Waterside station for the 11:15 train to Belfast (York Road). In hindsight, perhaps we should've caught a Swilly bus to Letterkenny to see the CDR and LLSR railway legacy (and further gems in the LLSR bus fleet) and travelled to Belfast later in the day, but we had probably advised our estimated arrival time at the Botanic Hotel in Botanic Avenue. The rail journey on the 11:15 included one amusing incident. The single line sections of the Northern Counties route were equipped with Manson's Apparatus tablet catchers, but, as we passed Cullybackey, north of

Ballymena, the MPD diesel came to a sudden stand. The tablet pouch for the section south, at the end of the loop, had not been correctly collected, bouncing off to come to rest in a lineside field. The diesel was immediately set back allowing the guard to retrieve the tablet with minimal time lost! After depositing the luggage at the hotel, we soon headed out into the city, looking at Oxford Street bus station, which contained a line-up of UTA half-cab Leyland PS1s, all withdrawn, parked on what had been the Harbour line tracks. Crossing the river to Queen's Quay station, we journeyed to Bangor by multi-engined diesel railcar (MED) over what had become an isolated part of the UTA rail network. My diary records Bangor as "a pleasant resort".

The next day was to be devoted to the Belfast trolleybus system, but first we visited York Road station and were able to observe from the footbridge crossing all lines, the loco shed containing an ex-GNR 0-6-0 (probably No 48 that had recently been steamed for a final time), the 4-4-0 No 171 *Slieve Gullion* now preserved and a selection of the 'Jeep' 2-6-4Ts of LMS (NCC) origin. *Lough Erne*, unfortunately devoid of one buffer, was again engaged in its usual station pilot duties. Heading along the Shore Road (at that time still a stone's throw from Belfast Lough), we photographed the red and cream six-wheel trolleybuses on the frequent cross-city Whitewell service. A surprise was finding a Southdown all-Leyland Leyland PD2 (LUF 228), which had latterly been Portsmouth allocated, at the Whitehouse Service Station. It had probably just arrived at the docks and would later be reported with Reliant Fabrics as a staff bus. From Whitewell we returned on the service 13 trolleybus to Glen Road terminus via the Falls Road. We walked back to the City Cemetery, passing Falls Park depot, which no longer had a trolleybus allocation, and caught an 11 up to Whiterock Road, a late wiring extension

to the trolleybus system. The local youngsters, no more than six- or seven-years-old, still commandeered the platform of every No 11 trolleybus as it arrived at the terminus, swinging around the stanchion pole until the last possible moment when kicked off by the conductor as the vehicle accelerated away. Their chorus to intending passengers was, "Will you give me two-pence, mister?"

From the city centre, we walked over to the large open-air Haymarket depot with its rows of withdrawn trolleybuses, mostly out of use since the loss of the Antrim Road routes. It was situated adjacent to the present Belfast Central station site, but in 1967 there was no longer a rail link between the former Great Northern, Co Down and NCC sections; the passenger link between the BCDR and GNR and Queen's Quay (Belfast Central Railway) ceased as long ago as November 1885 and until final closure it had been goods only except for very occasional passenger excursions between the GNR and BCDR. Once again, Haymarket depot staff welcomed us and allowed us to wander freely around the open parking areas.

We knew nothing of the ceremonies traditionally (and controversially) taking place on 12 July, when we intended travelling by The Enterprise to Dublin, but delayed departure to observe the spectacular sight of the Orangemen's Walk through the centre of Belfast. We were but casual observers, without knowledge of Ulster politics, but were impressed by the maces being tossed high enough to pass between positive and negative trolleybus wires. As all city centre bus services were suspended for the duration, the power was probably cut off as a precaution. As the walkers headed to the Finaghy 'Demonstration' for the afternoon, we headed from Great Victoria Street to Dublin (where Amiens Street was now re-named Connolly) aboard an ex-GN diesel set. En route, as we left Belfast, we noted withdrawn steam locomotives at Grosvenor Road and the closed Adelaide shed. Also seen from the train were an ex-Eastern Scottish AEC Regent III/ Duple with Farran (contractor), Dunmurry and a former Southdown Leyland Royal Tiger touring coach parked at Laytown (for Bettystown). After finding the Othello Hotel in Dublin, we spent the rest of the day wandering the city streets, having tea and a meal at Bewley's in Westmoreland Street, with its spectacular coloured glass roof lights. We had both studied James Joyce at school for 'A' level so many locations had a strange familiarity from *Portrait of the Artist as a Young Man* and *Ulysses*. City bus services were still worked by R or RA-class Leyland Titans with a few P and U-class single-deckers. Leyland Atlanteans of the D class, which had replaced ex GNR(I) AEC Regents and early post-war CIÉ Leylands, were in evidence but they were proving troublesome. On the following day, we went to Bray by bus – R545, a converted airport Leyland OPD2 – and later continued by train (a Park Royal-style railcar) through the Vale of Avoca to Arklow. Another ex-Southdown touring coach of the same batch (still registered LCD 205) was parked in the goods yard, visiting from its new operator at Navan. After looking at the town, we returned on another railcar set to Dublin where, in the evening, we walked to Heuston station as a trial run for the following morning, when we would depart from the terminus on the 09:35 to Waterford (Plunkett). This was loco-hauled, as were most CIÉ main line services at the time.

We crossed the river to Waterford Quay (from where Suir Way services departed with a couple of North Western Road Car single-deckers amongst others) and, after taking lunch, found we needed Kenneally's bus (an ex-London RTL Leyland PD2) to travel to the location of our accommodation, a pleasantly-appointed *pension* run by an Irish-Canadian lady. She thought George must be a printer as she had a nephew in that profession with similar handwriting! We spent the afternoon at Tramore, travelling there and back on AA 1, one of the rail replacement AEC Regent V double-deckers with additional luggage space. At that time, much of the roadside section of the isolated branch was clearly visible and the station building was easily found. This was poignant as we both knew a colleague in the staff section of the Divisional Manager's Office at Wimbledon, Eddie McGuirk, who had been on the staff at Tramore in his earlier CIÉ career.

A hearty breakfast at the *pension* on the following morning was nearly thwarted by a sudden piercing hoot from a ship on the River Suir behind the house which almost caused the proprietress to drop the breakfast tray in alarm. Following one more journey on Kenneally's RTL, we joined the 11:05 from Waterford, behind locomotive B104, to Limerick Junction with its curious layout necessitating reversals for almost every train, and connected there for Cork via Mallow, where a small tank engine (No 90) was preserved on a plinth. Similarly, an early Great Southern and Western Railway engine occupied a prominent position on the concourse at Cork, now called Kent but formerly Glanmire Road. The journey from Waterford would've been more interesting and direct if we had taken the line to Mallow via Dungarvan, but the service was sparse and we were unaware it would close before long.

We settled in at the Windsor Hotel in Cork's McCurtain Street, which was convenient for rail passengers. The following day was an extremely wet Sunday. We were surprised to find at breakfast a school friend staying at the same hotel, having voyaged from Southampton to Cobh on the liner *Queen Mary*. The morning was spent travelling to Cobh on another GNR(I) pattern railcar, but, as we came to a stand in the platform, smoke started rising from beneath the floor. Station and train staff rapidly produced fire extinguishers and had the fire out before the local fire brigade arrived. The afternoon was spent at Blarney castle, reached on R680, one of the small batch of CIÉ PD2s used on Cork City services. However, in the pouring rain, I declined the option of adopting a contortionist's pose to kiss the Blarney Stone! In the evening I walked to Tivoli while George went to Youghal on one of the occasional excursion trains over a line officially closed.

Leaving Cork on the following morning up the arduous gradient partially in tunnel, we were bound for Galway (Ceannt), involving changes at Limerick Junction, Limerick and Athenry on what was another very wet morning. The carriage on the train from Limerick featured double doors which slid back between corridor and compartment, which we shared with two middle-aged ladies and a priest who smoked a cigarette despite being in a non-smoker! The Limerick connectional time was spent in the buffet as the deluge had worsened at that point. Our train called at Ennis, formerly junction for the West Clare Railway and the last of that line's tank engines was visible under a canopy on the platform. At Athenry, where we had a lengthy connection of several hours, two boxes of day-old chicks were offloaded from our train and promptly delivered to the consignee by the junior porter, who pedalled off furiously on the station bicycle with the livestock parcels conveyed in the pannier basket over the front wheel.

Giblin's Hotel was found to be conveniently situated opposite Galway station in Eyre Square and, although primarily a noisy bar, it specially provided an excellent early breakfast on the following morning as we needed to catch a train at 09:30. Unexpected at the hotel was a dog kennel (empty) on the landing and a sighting of a herd of heifers passing across Eyre Square 'on the hoof'! No doubt they had

just been offloaded from a few of CIÉ's multitude of cattle wagons in the station goods yard. Our evening in Galway included a bus ride to the resort of Salthill, travelling on PD2s in both directions. Arriving at the ticket office in good time to purchase our privilege tickets on the following morning, we found the clerk taken aback at seeing BR documents, but he was eager to tell us he had heard of Waterloo. The 09:30 train conveyed us to Athlone, where we changed for Mullingar, making a further connection to Sligo. At both intermediate locations, we had several hours to wait so there was time to inspect the town. The wide river at Athlone was viewed, as was an ex-Smith of Reading Bedford SB (NUR 17), still in blue and orange, parked without identification of the new owner, while memories of Mullingar include donkey carts waiting patiently for their owners outside bars in the main street.

Accommodation in Sligo had been booked at the Bonne Chère Guest House – a most comfortable location charging only 18/6 (92½p) for bed and breakfast – a remarkable bargain even in 1967. We had to cross the road to their associated restaurant for breakfast, but that was no hardship. An ex-Western National Bristol LS coach (owned by Dublin Hire Coaches) and an ex-Whittle of Highley Bedford SB were the only non-CIÉ vehicles noted in Sligo, but at the depot there was a line-up of P class Leyland Tiger half-cabs, still in use. Following an overnight stay and morning walk around the town, we departed Sligo (MacDiamarda) at 13:35 for Dublin for a further overnight stay at the Othello Hotel. The guard on this service noted our interest and explained the automatic tablet exchange and bell code system. After a meal at Bewley's, we caught a CIÉ RA class PD3 to Dun Laoghaire, returning by train after noting the port facilities and train shed, then still rail connected.

The 11:00 Enterprise from Connolly conveyed us back to Belfast (Great Victoria Street) on the following morning (Thursday 20th). A rake of very elderly panelled carriages attracted our attention in a siding just north of Connolly while an ex-Maidstone and District Harrington-bodied AEC coach, still in cream and holly green, was noted at the lineside in Lurgan and at least five Scottish AEC Regals were now parked in Farran's yard at Dunmurry. The luggage was quickly deposited at the Botanic Hotel, enabling us to spend the afternoon inspecting the remarkable collection of exhibits crammed into such a limited space at the Witham Street Transport Musuem. Surviving gems included vehicles from the Giant's Causeway, Bessbrook and Newry, County Donegal and trams from the Belfast municipal system. Travel to Witham Street was on a Corporation Guy Arab III/Harkness and the return along the Newtownards Road was on one of the MH Coachworks-bodied Daimler Fleetlines that had taken over on the East Belfast trolleybus routes. There was still time before an evening meal to make a trolleybus journey up to Whitewell and back to Castle Junction.

Our Irish interlude was almost at an end and we left the Botanic Hotel for a twenty-three hour journey back to Portsmouth, commencing with a short journey to City Hall on a rebodied wartime Daimler CWA6 and a service 10 trolleybus to York Road (NCC) station. An MPD railcar set conveyed us to Larne Harbour where *Caledonian Princess* was again the vessel on the Stranraer crossing. A diesel multiple unit conveyed us across the bleak moorland terrain of Wigtownshire and to Glasgow, from where we would travel on an overnight service to Euston, and thence from Waterloo, which no longer resounded to Bournemouth line steam, on a Portsmouth line electric.

I made one more journey to see Belfast's trolleybuses in their death throes on what was an extended day. By May 1968 I was working in the Divisional Manager's office at Wimbledon (still on the railway studentship scheme)

Duke of Rothesay at Heysham

so headed to Waterloo from work for tea in the civilised surroundings of the Windsor Rooms, long swept away. I then joined the Ulster Boat Express at Euston for Heysham Harbour where *Duke of Rothesay* was the vessel on the night crossing. A seat was obtained in the lounge but my diary records "usual conditions" for the night crossing was to be endured rather than enjoyed. Arriving at Belfast's Donegall Quay somewhat late (at 08:00), first call was for breakfast before travelling commenced with a journey along the Shore Road to Whitewell – by now construction of the M2 motorway had begun so the Lough was further away. I returned to the Falls Road, also travelling over the Glen Road and Whiterock Road branches. Many of the surviving active trolleybuses were visibly rundown by now and some were even running with tow plates missing, as if ready to be dragged to Beattie's scrapyard at Hillsborough.

At Haymarket depot, the unique four-wheel Sunbeam (No 246) was being driven around the depot circuit by Tony Belton who had saved it for preservation. The Corporation had overhauled and repainted the five trolleybuses secured for preservation – Nos 98, 112, 168, 183 and 246 – and these sparkled by contrast with their doomed sister vehicles. No 98 stood at the depot, but this trolleybus, the last AEC 664T, although destined for the Transport Museum, would be allowed to deteriorate out of the public eye and is in storage. No 246 was about to leave on a tour of the system so we were invited to join the small group to make final visits to Falls Road and Whitewell, as well as the depot-only wiring to and from City Hall. With authority, I managed to acquire a destination screen from a withdrawn trolleybus at Haymarket and carried that back to Portsmouth. My final journey on a trolleybus in Belfast was on No 231, to York Road station for the train to Larne Harbour and the crossing to Stranraer aboard the new vessel *Antrim Princess*. The trolleybus system would close the following day (12 May), with several of the vehicles to be preserved conveying the official party, but I had experienced it on the penultimate day.

In addition to my 1967 photographs, some from the 1965 visit and the 1968 day excursion have been included, for there had been a few major changes in the bus fleets during the intervening years.

It would be almost twenty years before my next holiday in Ireland – although there was a day trip to Dublin from the Isle of Man aboard the SS *King Orry* in the mid 1970s. The subsequent visits were for the May weekend railtours behind the preserved steam locomotives of the Railway Preservation Society of Ireland. By the time I reached Northern Ireland again, the classic vehicles to be photographed and travelled upon were Leyland Leopards and Bristol RELLs.

I'm grateful to Colourpoint Books for agreeing to publish a further edition of *Irish Buses in the mid-1960s* covering more of my photographic efforts depicting Irish buses and trolleybuses. Much of the caption enhancement is the work of Paul Savage whose superior local knowledge of the transport system past and present has proved invaluable. I am also grateful to him for preparing the draft in readiness for publication. Finally, I must also thank Howard Cunningham, Cyril McIntyre and Jonathan Miller for casting a critical eye and offering enhancements to a number of captions.

I hope you will enjoy this third volume in Colourpoint's Irish Bus Photographers series.

Richard Newman
Portsmouth
May 2018

BELFAST CORPORATION

We begin our look at Belfast Corporation with a view of Daimler CWA6 No 500 (HGF 869) in Donegall Square West on 26 July 1965. In 1953, the Corporation bought from North's, Leeds, 100 of these former London Transport wartime Daimlers to hasten the abandonment of the tramway system, which was completed in 1954. After repaint and the fitting of a Belfast destination layout, many ran with the utility bodies with which they arrived before all were re-bodied locally by the Belfast firm, Harkness, which supplied many bus bodies to Belfast Corporation up to 1963. No 500 is on service 22 to Parliament Buildings via Queen's Bridge, which had been a trolleybus route until 1963.

No 243 (GZ 3992), seen in Donegall Square West en route to Holywood Road on 26 July 1965, is a Daimler CVA6, again bodied by Harkness. It was new in 1946 and served the city for a creditable twenty-one years, being withdrawn in 1967. The Holywood Road route also saw trolleybus operation, but only for a short time, between November 1952 and June 1958. No 243 carries the reduced depth destination and via blinds introduced with the conversion of trolleybus routes to diesel bus operation.

Having just rounded the roundabout at the Falls Road/Kennedy Way junction in the west of the city, and with the crane at Eastwood's scrapyard to be seen just to the rear of the trolleybus, Guy BTX No 156 (GZ 8520) heads towards the Falls Road terminus at Casement Park on 26 July 1965.

With the gates to Milltown cemetery to the right of the picture, BUT9641T trolleybus No 198 (GZ 8562) was photographed on 26 July 1965 at the Falls Road/Glen Road roundabout outside Falls depot though, by this time, the depot was not used by trolleybuses. The road layout here is to change significantly with the removal of the roundabout and its replacement with a traffic light-controlled junction in preparation for the introduction in August 2018 of the bus-based Belfast Rapid Transit system, Glider.

This is the terminus at Whitewell, in the north of the city, looking across Belfast Lough to the Co Down side. New in 1948, No 108 (FZ 7893) is a Guy BTX and gave the city twenty years' service.

In 1952/3, the Corporation took delivery of its first eight-foot wide buses, 100 Daimler CVs, 98 of them Gardner-engined, with exposed radiators (Nos 350–447) and two Daimler-engined examples (Nos 448/9), which had tin fronts. These vehicles were intended for tramway replacement. No 408 (OZ 6662) is seen in Great Victoria Street on service 77 to the Gasworks 26 July 1965.

Service 77, which ran from the Waterworks, in the north of the city, to the Gasworks, in the south, was an unusual cross-city service as it only touched the edge of the central area. It was also a very busy service, with a high frequency. The 77 crossed both the Falls Road and Shankill Road and the violence which erupted in 1969 and the disruption and destruction caused, led ultimately to the withdrawal of this useful, and popular, route. Daimler CVG6 No 401 (OZ 6655) is crossing the Boyne Bridge, over the railway tracks at Great Victoria Street station, en route to the Gasworks on 26 July 1965.

Another view of a Daimler CVG6 on service 77 to the Gasworks, this time No 394 (OZ 6648), pictured on Great Victoria Street the following day, 27 July 1965. No 394 transferred to Citybus Ltd in April 1973, on the takeover of the Corporation's bus services, and was withdrawn the same year.

BUT9641T No 223 (OZ 7325) looks most presentable as it heads for Fortwilliam on service 8. Trolleybuses on Shore Road routes could also turn short at Grove. No 223 is passing St Paul's church on York Road on 27 July 1965, the Ulster Transport Authority railway station being behind and to the left of the photographer.

Just visible behind trolleybus No 223 in the previous picture is Daimler Fleetline No 639 (639 EZ) on York Road heading for Greencastle on service 7 from Turf Lodge. The Shore Road was served at this time by trolleybuses working through from the Falls Road routes and diesel buses working cross-city from Turf Lodge via the Springfield Road, this road never having been wired for trolleybuses.

BUT9641T trolleybus No 200 (GZ 8564) sits on the siding outside York Road station waiting for passengers to arrive off the Stranraer–Larne boat train on 27 July 1965. The destination display shows Grove Park as the trolleybus would have run to that point before returning to the station siding. Beyond the trolleybus is an electric truck belonging to the Belfast Co-operative Wholesale Society.

With the railway station to the left in this view, BUT9641T 215 (OZ 7317) on service 8 to Fortwilliam passes along York Road on 27 July 1965. Note the perfectly set route number, destination and via displays, though the last is actually listed in reverse order for this direction of travel. I doubt that would be Disability Discrimination Act-compliant as intermediate stopping points are now often omitted to avoid confusion!

En route from Downview in the northern suburbs to Ormeau in the south and seen passing York Road railway station is Guy Arab III No 349 (MZ 7447), which dates from 1951 and the last of the batch of 45 similar vehicles. It's overtaking BUT9641T trolleybus No 200 (GZ 8564) outside York Road railway station 27 July 1965. The observant reader will notice that No 200 has had its destination screen re-set to City Hall!

Now preserved at the National Transport Museum at Howth, just outside Dublin, Guy BTX trolleybus No 183 (GZ 8547) is seen passing York Road station, en route to Glen Road, on 27 July 1965. It is being overtaken by a Leyland PD3/4 from the Ulster Transport Authority fleet. The 'via' screen is of interest showing 'passes Northern Counties Railway', though no mention of serving the Falls Road!

BUT9641T trolleybus No 231 (OZ 7333), heading for Whitewell, passes along York Road on route 10 on 27 July 1965. No 231 survived until the closure of the system in 1968.

Citybound on East Bridge Street on 28 July 1965, Daimler CVA6 No 277 (GZ 4031) has just passed the exit from Haymarket depot on its way to the city centre.

No 227 (GZ 2675), seen on Short Strand on 28 July 1965, just after leaving the depot, is a wartime Daimler CWA6, which was rebodied by Harkness in 1951 and which still looked smart, when photographed, for its fourteen years. New in 1945, No 227 gave the Corporation twenty-four years' service, being withdrawn in 1969 after suffering damage in an accident.

In 1963, the Corporation took delivery of its first batch of front entrance, rear-engined double-deckers in the form of 88 Gardner-engined Daimler Fleetlines, numbered 553–640. These were bodied not by Harkness, but by a new company, MH Coachworks, based at Dunmore, in the north of the city. The chassis for this batch arrived complete, but those for the following order, Nos 641–703, arrived completely knocked down, being assembled by the associated MH Cars and resulting in a product constructed entirely in the city. No 554 (554 EZ) is seen crossing the Albert Bridge en route from Bloomfield to the city centre 28 July 1965. The trolleybus service to Bloomfield was replaced with diesel buses after 13 October 1963.

During the damp evening peak hour on 28 July 1965, Daimler CVA6 No 279 (GZ 4033), the last of the batch, crosses the Albert Bridge en route to City Hall. The single-track route number blinds ran from 1 to 99 so pity a driver changing from, for example, a low-numbered Antrim Road route (1–6) to works specials 97–99! No 279 served from 1947 to 1969.

The penultimate member of this batch of Harkness-bodied Daimler CVA6s, No 278 (GZ 4032), was photographed just after similar No 279, also on the Albert Bridge, when en route from Ravenhill to the city centre. Note the power feeder cables for the trolleybus overhead above No 278. The houses visible to the left of the picture, on the far side of the bridge, are in the Short Strand area.

On a short working from Mount Merrion, Daimler CVA6 No 241 (GZ 3990) stops to pick up a passenger in Botanic Avenue on 28 July 1965. She might be in for a surprise as, if the destination of Shaftesbury Square is correct, then the bus will serve just one more stop!

Citybound from the Ormeau Road, Daimler CWA6 No 480 (GYL 276), previously London Transport D111, was photographed in Botanic Avenue on 28 July 1965. Belfast's impressive Botanic Gardens, with its palm house and tropical ravine, are situated a short distance further along the road.

In 1950, Belfast Corporation took delivery of a batch of 25 Guy Arab III single-deckers with Harkness bodies. No 290 (MZ 7388), seen on Queen's Quay on 28 July 1965, was one of just a few to see a full service life, not being withdrawn until 1970; Nos 292–7 were withdrawn and sold in 1958 and six others were converted to grit spreaders in 1962/4.

Three days later on Queen's Quay and Daimler CWA6 No 454 (GLX 902) on service 51 *from* Queen's Road heads to the city centre, passing the railway station at Queen's Quay, by then only serving trains to Bangor, after the closure of most of the former Belfast and Co Down Railway network in 1950. The roadworks are associated with the building of the flyover at Station Street.

Daimler CVG6 No 401 (OZ 6655), pictured earlier (page 17) in the week on route 77, was photographed again, crossing the Queen's Bridge this time, on 31 July 1965. The route number 24 and the destination Bloomfield are a mis-match, the 24 running from the Braniel estate.

A further 63 Daimler Fleetlines, again with MH Coachworks bodies, were delivered in 1964. No 688 (688 FZ) arrives at the Glen Road terminus of the Turf Lodge via Springfield Road route on 11 July 1967, having run cross-town from the Shore Road. Behind the bus is St Teresa's church.

With St Teresa's church to the left, BUT9641T No 205 (GZ 8569) and Guy BTX No 189 (GZ 8553) approach Glen Road terminus on 11 July 1967. The observant may notice on the trolleybus standard to the right, an Ulster Transport Authority bus stop for service 105 to Stoneyford via Sales Corner.

Seen earlier, in a 1965 view on York Road (page 21), BUT9641T No 231 (OZ 7333) is pictured here on 11 July 1967 on the other side of the city, leaving Glen Road terminus as Guy BTX No 189 arrives. Both of the trolleybuses were still around in 1968.

Trolleybus No 179 (GZ 8543), another Guy BTX, with electrical equipment by GEC, is seen on the same day as the previous photograph, countrybound on Glen Road.

Guy BTX No 127 (FZ 7912), which was new in 1948 and went on to serve the city for twenty years, was photographed at the Whiterock terminus on 11 July 1967.

This is East Bridge Street, approaching Cromac Square, in the Markets district close to the city centre, on 11 July 1967. No 474 (GYE 77) is another of the 100 former London Transport Daimler CWA6s and was previously D87 in that fleet. Queen's Bridge routes would not normally pass this point so perhaps the driver has already set the blinds for his next trip. The building to the left of the picture is the Corporation's St George's Market, now a popular venue on Fridays, Saturdays and Sundays for local produce, speciality foods, arts, crafts and collectables. The road rising to the right, over the former Belfast Central Railway, is the continuation of East Bridge Street, where the scene in 2018 is very much changed.

Seen in Royal Avenue on 20 July 1967, Daimler CWA6 No 522 (HGC 289) is en route to take up a service 70 journey to Cavehill Road via York Street and Limestone Road. Cavehill Road was the terminus for the Corporation's first motorbus route in October 1926.

After my travels around Ireland, I was back in Belfast on 20 July 1967 to photograph Guy BTX Trolleybus No 123 (FZ 7908) climbing Whitewell Road towards the terminus. This section had earlier to be taken at minimal speed as a section of running wire had become detached from the span wire.

The next arrival at the Whitewell terminus, on the north side of the city overlooking Belfast Lough, was BUT9641T No 194 (GZ 8558). This view, with the terminus a short distance behind the photographer, also dates from 20 July 1967, less than 10 months before the trolleybuses would all be gone.

This is the square-setted terminus at St Teresa's on the Glen Road with Daimler Fleetline No 727 (727 UZ), with stylish Alexander-inspired bodywork by Belfast firm Potter's, about to depart cross-city to Greencastle on service 7 on 11 May 1968. The Greencastle route along the Shore Road had been served by trolleybuses between October 1950 and May 1962, its picking-up and setting down arrangements being the cause of some dispute between the Corporation and the Ulster Transport Authority.

Guy BTX trolleybus No 121 (FZ 7906) is shown here on Royal Avenue on 11 May 1968, the penultimate day of trolleybus operation. It's on route 12 to the Falls Road terminus at Casement Park and will have been running cross-city from the Shore Road.

11 May 1968 and former London Transport Daimler CWA6s Nos 539 (HGC 278) followed by 536 (HGC 264) awaited departure time in Donegall Square West on routes to the east of the city. No 539 is on service 76 to Gilnahirk via the Albert Bridge and No 536 is heading for Braniel via the Queen's Bridge. Having followed different routes out of the city centre, they might just meet again on the common section between the Ropeworks corner and the Sandown Road.

On 11 May 1968, the day before the system closed, I was permitted a visit to the depot at Haymarket where Guy BTX No 125 (FZ 7910) lay withdrawn and awaiting disposal.

The Corporation took delivery of its first single-deckers suitable for one-man-operation (and it would've been one <u>man</u> at that time!) in 1968, though they were stored, pending negotiations, until 1969; some, though, did see use on private hire. Two types, both bodied locally by Potters, successor to MH Coachworks, were taken into stock – dual-door Daimler Roadliners and single-door AEC Swifts. One of the former, No 740 (740 UZ) and ex Ulster Transport Authority Leyland PS1 B8686 (MZ 357), withdrawn in 1962, then sold to the Corporation and converted to a mobile public library, are seen at Haymarket on 11 May 1968; another UTA Leyland PS1, B8726 (MZ 397), was similarly converted at the same time. A further Corporation mobile public library was converted in 1964 from one of its own Harkness-bodied Guy Arab IIIs, No 289.

Daimler CVA6 No 242 (GZ 3991) and Guy BTX trolleybus No 191 (GZ 8555) at Haymarket depot awaiting disposal on 11 May 1968. No 242 had served twenty-one years, from 1946 to 1967, No 191 eighteen years, from 1950 to 1968.

CÓRAS IOMPAIR ÉIREANN

Photographed on 29 July 1965, just after the author arrived from Belfast at Amiens Street station, Leyland OPD2 'Standard' R288 (ZD 7178), new in 1948, heads along Amiens Street towards Dollymount. It gave CIÉ twenty years' service. Behind the bus are the offices of Ashenhurst Williams, the main Leyland dealer.

At Dublin's Store Street bus station, now better known as Busáras, Leyland Royal Tiger PSU1/13 U61, with 45-seat rear entrance CIÉ-built bodywork, loads passengers for an unknown destination on 29 July 1965. U51–70 were built for provincial services, with ladders to the rear roof rack, U71–88 for Dublin city services. All were later rebuilt with front or, in some cases, dual doors.

Seen on Store Street, is Leyland Tiger OPS3/1 P26 (ZD 7166), new in 1948 with 39-seat, front entrance bodywork built by CIÉ. The lack of luggage space made this batch (P1–30) less than useful for use on provincial services, given the amount of luggage often carried, though a number later had roof-mounted luggage racks fitted. P26 had a varied working life. After provincial service, in 1952 it was fitted with 30 coach seats for use on the service between the city centre and Dublin airport, but this lasted just a year before it was transferred to city services joining P1–25. The narrow entrance and high floor made the type less than ideal for city use. P26 was also experimentally fitted with air suspension and ended its working life converted to a garage towing tender at Phibsboro.

The RA class was built on the Leyland Titan PD3/2 chassis, the first entering service in 1959. The class totalled 152 when deliveries were completed in 1961. RA82 (OYI 847) was photographed on 29 July 1965 on Dublin city service, heading for Nelson Pillar, which would be blown up the following year. The bus had acquired the monastral blue and cream livery, first introduced on RA137 in 1961.

Similar RA45 (OYI 810), seen on O'Connell Street the same day, with the Nelson Pillar in the background, wore the two-tone green livery, with the CIÉ 'winged wheel' emblem. It had also acquired a replacement radiator grille. The last members of the class ran in service in 1982.

In 1953, the Great Northern Railway built a batch of nine eight-foot wide, Park Royal-framed bodies on AEC Regent III 9621Es. They were numbered 299–307 and were prefixed AR when taken into the CIÉ fleet in 1958. AR303 (ZU 3142) was photographed on Amiens Street on 29 July 1965. The platform doors were fitted from new.

AR292 (IY 5394) is an older AEC Regent III, an O961 model, new in 1948 with eight-foot wide body built at Dundalk by the Great Northern on Park Royal frames. Several members of the batch gave twenty years' service, not being withdrawn until 1968. AR292 is seen on Amiens Street, en route to St Anne's, on 29 July 1965.

A410 (ZH 3909) is an AEC Regal Mark III 0962, one of 24 new to the Great Northern Railway in 1948 and taken over by CIÉ ten years later. The 39-seat bodywork was built by Park Royal on Metal Sections frames. This view was taken at Store Street bus station on 29 July 1965 when A410 was on the Cavan service.

In this general view of Lower Leeson Street on 29 July 1965 we can see the tram track on the hump bridge over the Grand Canal, which is about to be crossed by Leyland OPD2/1 R543, one of six similar vehicles built at Spa Road works in 1953 for use on the airport service. When new, they featured full-front bodies, coach seats and a large rear luggage compartment. They were rebuilt in 1964/5 and withdrawn in 1974.

This is Donnybrook garage on 30 July 1965 and Leyland Tiger OPS3/1s
P21 (ZD 7161), P26 (ZD 7166) and P217 (ZJ 5957) await their next turns
of duty. The first two are from the 1948 batch, the last from the 1951.
P217 also differs from the other two by having a rear-entrance Spa
Road-built CIÉ body.

Also at Donnybrook is garage tender H5 (ZD 3654), a Leyland TS11 new in 1947, though the chassis had been delivered to the Great Southern Railway in 1942. H5 had been numbered T21 when a bus and was registered ZD 949. On conversion to a garage tender, it ran on trade plate 062 ZC, but a change of policy in the 1960s saw such vehicles taxed with their original numbers. H5 was an exception as it somehow received the number previously carried by similar TS11 T6 (ZD 3654), which had been tender H7.

Again in the shed at Donnybrook, we see Leyland OPD2/1 R542 (ZO 6961), one of the six similar vehicles built at Spa Road works in 1953 for use on the airport service, and Leyland Tiger OPS3/1 P216 (ZJ 5956) and P200 (ZJ 5940).

Still on the south side of the city, but back towards the centre as we see Leyland PD2/3 R397 (ZJ 1357) on service 5, followed by Leyland PD3/2 RA2 (CYI 637) on service 7a in Merrion Square North on 12 July 1967. Note that R397, of the Capetown class, is now displaying O'Connell Street as the destination, rather than Nelson Pillar which had been destroyed by a bomb in 1966.

The following day, R276 (ZD 991) was seen on city route 62 at Burgh Quay. R276 was one of 20 Leyland OPD1s (R261–80), which entered service in 1946/7 as CIÉ's first new Leyland double-deckers. They were eight feet wide and just over 27 feet long and were christened the 'Queen Mary' type by crews. The wide pillar separating the upper deck front window panes may be noted. This simple expedient was a way of using up glass stocks intended for narrower vehicles. Similarly, one bay in the side was longer than the rest. In 1963/4, the mechanical specification was upgraded making them effectively OPD2s, with much improved performance.

Also on Burgh Quay on 13 July 1967 is Leyland PD3/2 RA34 (CYI 669), after arrival on route 55 from Blackrock and Cabinteely.

In 1954/5, the Great Northern Railway placed in service 33 AEC Regal Mark IV 9822E buses and coaches, all with bodywork built in-house, and they were the last new buses placed in service by the GNR. All passed to CIÉ in 1958. Here we see ex-GNR 267 (ZY 490), as CIÉ AU267, rebuilt with front entrance and fitted for one-man operation, at Store Street bus station on 13 July 1967, ready to depart for Monaghan (Muineachán).

To Waterford now where Leyland OPD1 R275 (ZD 990) is seen on Parade Quay on its way to Sliabh Caol on 14 July 1967. R275 entered service on Dublin city routes and can be identified as a 1946 delivery by having half-drop windows in the CIÉ's Spa Road works-built body; the 1947 deliveries had sliding windows. The batch of 20, R261–80, was unpopular when new, due to poor performance, but was upgraded to OPD2 specification in 1963/4 and gave good service, including, as seen here, at provincial garages.

CIÉ-bodied, on Metal Sections frames, Leyland Leopard C10 (EZH 10) and Leyland OPD1 R271 (ZD 986) were photographed parked up on Parade Quay, later the same day. The Leopard was a PSU3/4R model with 45 bus seats and was new in 1965.

Back to Dublin, and heading along Amiens Street on route 30 to Dollymount on 20 July 1967 is Leyland OPD2/1 R290 (ZD 7180), the last member of the batch of ten (R281–90) delivered in 1948. When new, R290 was the first Leyland bus in the fleet to have a chromed radiator shell, but by 1967 that had obviously been replaced. Also, when new, R290 was allocated to Donnybrook, but was almost certainly working from Clontarf garage when photographed.

Clontarf-allocated R627 (JRI 57), seen on route 54 passing along Amiens Street, Dublin, on 20 July 1967, is a Leyland OPD2/1 new in 1956 and known to operating staff as Standards. Some survived in service until early 1976. The batch, R581–650, was the first batch of CIÉ buses to be given three-letter registration numbers

INDEPENDENTS

In 1966, the Ulster Transport Authority gave up some unremunerative routes in the Lurgan and Portrush areas, the former passing to Sureline Coaches; the latter passed to Coastal Bus Service of Portrush. Leyland Royal Tiger PSU1/9 JWO 122, with Lydney bodywork, was previously Red & White, Chepstow, U2.51 and joined the Coastal fleet, as No 4, in May 1967, remaining until closure and sale to Ulsterbus in April 1974. It was photographed in the station yard, Portrush, on the Ballycastle service on 8 July 1967.

Coastal Bus Service, Portrush No 7 (EHE 940), a Willowbrook-bodied Leyland Royal Tiger PSU1/13, new to Yorkshire Traction, Barnsley as its No 993, joined the North Antrim coast fleet in August 1966 when thirteen years old. ECK 586, another Leyland Royal Tiger PSU1/13, though Leyland-bodied, was ex-Ribble Motor Services No 323 and was one of the first vehicles acquired in April 1966. It was numbered 3 and passed to Ulsterbus as its No 9040 in April 1974. The location for this view is the garage at Dunluce Avenue, Portrush, which was former Ulster Transport Authority premises. The notices on the beam refer to the parking of the Authority's Royal Tigers, which had roof racks so wouldn't fit.

The Londonderry and Lough Swilly Railway Company began operation of bus services in 1929 and continued to serve much of north County Donegal until closure in 2014. A particularly interesting acquisition in 1960 was from Leyland Motors, making Lough Swilly company one of the first operators in Ireland to own the revolutionary rear-engined Atlantean model. Numbered 87, this 1959 model had originally run in Great Britain registered 46 LTB, then 8895 XI when demonstrated to the Ulster Transport Authority before becoming HZA 723 when trialled by Córas Iompair Éireann. It gained its fourth registration in number, UI 8616, when put into Swilly service in July 1960. It is seen here on Foyle Road seven years later, on 8 July 1967. It survived until September 1980, when it entered preservation, but it was later sold for scrap.

Lough Swilly No 64 (UI 4291) was a Leyland PS2/1 new in 1949 with 34-seat, rear entrance bodywork built by the Ulster Transport Authority. It had been withdrawn by June 1964 and was dumped at Pennyburn, where, like many Swilly vehicles, it became a source of parts. This view was taken on 9 July 1967 and No 64 was scrapped about four months later.

Being from Portsmouth, the photographer was pleased no end by the sight of former Southdown Motor Services vehicles in faraway Derry and Donegal. Lough Swilly No 104 (LUF 607) seen at Pennyburn on 9 July 1967, had been numbered 1607 in the Southdown fleet and reached the Swilly in December 1964, when about twelve and a half years old, via Ascough (dealer), Dublin. It was withdrawn in 1974 and became a fisherman's hut at Rossnowlagh, Co Donegal.

As mentioned previously, many withdrawn buses ended their days at the Pennyburn headquarters as a source of spare parts to keep the rest of the fleet going, which could be difficult given the state of Donegal roads at the time. Here we see Nos 67 (UI 4294), 52 (IH 5709) and ex UTA Q181 (GZ 696) dumped at Pennyburn, 9 July 1967. No 67, a UTA-bodied Leyland PS2/1, had been new in 1949 and was withdrawn by June 1964. No 52 was an AEC Regal, new in June 1948 with a secondhand body built by the Great Southern Railway and later received an Ulster Transport Authority body removed from an Authority Leyland PS2; it had latterly been in use as a changing room at a Buncrana golf club after the clubhouse had burned down. Q181 had been acquired from the UTA in 1960 as a parts donor. It was an AEC Regal, new in 1936 to the Birmingham Co-operative Society, registered COA 999 before passing to the Royal Army Service Corps in 1942 then to the Northern Ireland Road Transport Board by 1943, where it received a new body in 1946.

No 56 (IH 6245) (left) was an AEC Regal, new in August 1948, with 35-seat bodywork by Eastern Coach Works and reputed to be part of a cancelled export order, though that has never been confirmed; it was obviously more expensive to bring a complete vehicle to Ireland, making this purchase more unusual. It ran until 1959 and lay disused at Pennyburn until at least 1967. No 45 (IH 5617) was a Leyland PS1, new in 1946. It was fitted then with a secondhand Alexander/DUTC body before it received this 1949 UTA body, removed from Leyland PS2 No C8769 (MZ 1840) in 1956/7. It was withdrawn from service in late 1963.

Leyland PS2/1 No 65 (UI 4292), new in 1949, and No 46, a Leyland PS1 new in 1946, both then withdrawn, rest beside a former railway carriage in use as a store at Pennyburn on 9 July 1967. No 65 had become Derry City FC's team coach in December 1964 before passing to St Columb's College, Derry, in 1968. Its final duties were as a fisherman's hut on Inishowen by May 1970. No 46 had a secondhand Alexander/DUTC body when new, but had received this UTA B34R from the Authority's Leyland PS2 No C8783 (MZ 1854) in 1956/7. It had been withdrawn in December 1963.

Between 1951 and 1953, the Swilly bought new eight Leyland Royal Tiger PSU1/9 with 44-seat, centre entrance Saunders-Roe bodies built on Anglesey. Nos 71–4 were registered in Co Donegal, 75–8 in Derry. No 74 (IH 9841), photographed at Pennyburn 9 July 1967, ran until 1974 when it was sold to Hollybush Primary School, Londonderry, where it was used as a music room.

December 1962 saw the purchase of four former North Western Road Car Co Ltd Leyland-bodied Royal Tiger PSU1/19 from Cowley, Salford (dealer). These were numbered 96–99 and received Derry registration numbers UI 9511–4. No 98, ex NWRCC 604 (FDB 604), is seen at Pennyburn on 9 July 1967.

Moving south from Derry sees us at Strabane, once a major railway centre where the standard gauge line of the Great Northern Railway and the narrow gauge line of the Co Donegal Railway met. The CDR lines had closed in 1961, the GNR, later UTA, in 1965. The CDR, like the Swilly before it, replaced its services with road transport for both passengers and freight. Initially, P class Leyland OPS3/1 and PS2/14 were hired from Córas Iompair Éireann, but in 1965 six former East Midland Motor Services Saro-bodied Leyland Tiger Cubs (ORR 321/2/31/2/3/9) were purchased. ORR 333, ex East Midland R333, was photographed in the Market Place, Strabane, on 9 July 1967.

To the diagonally-opposite end of the country now, to Waterford, where, in Lombard Street, we see Kenneally's Bus Service AWI 617, the former London Transport Leyland PD2 RTL 835 (KYY 805), working on the town service in July 1967.

ULSTER TRANSPORT AUTHORITY/ULSTERBUS

The Northern Ireland Road Transport Board and its successor, the Ulster Transport Authority, had a large number of 34-seat, rear entrance single-deckers, most with bodies built in-house on AEC Regal, Dennis Lancet and Leyland PS1 and 2 chassis. Here, at Great Victoria Street bus station 26 July 1965, we see Ulster Transport Authority Leyland PS1 No A568 (GZ 6121), waiting to depart on the local service 104 to Suffolk, to the west of the city. This vehicle was new in 1947 and the bodywork was built by the Northern Ireland Road Transport Board. It was the only standard PS1 to be officially absorbed into the Ulsterbus fleet in April 1967, but was withdrawn, following mechanical issues, the following October.

The Ulster Transport Authority took delivery of Leyland PD3/4s between 1959 and 1963, all with bodies built in-house on Metro-Cammell-Weymann frames. One of the 1961 deliveries, Q855 (8855 AZ), passes York Road station on 27 July 1965 when on service 161a to Rathcoole, once the largest public housing estate in Europe.

MZ 1810 was a Leyland PS1, which was new in 1948 as bus B8739 with the Authority's standard 34-seat, rear entrance bodywork, built in-house. Withdrawn from Enniskillen depot in 1963, where it had latterly been one of a number of vehicles painted in the colours of the erstwhile Erne Bus Service (Devenish Carriage & Wagon Co Ltd), it was converted as the Authority's 'Unit Wagon' and numbered B2796. It's seen here leaving York Road railway works on 27 July 1965.

To the yard at the rear of Oxford Street bus station now where on 28 July 1965 Leyland PS1s A572 (GZ 6125), Z7816 (GZ 4712) and A8549 (GZ 7617) are parked out of service, the first and last en route to Duncrue Street works for annual test preparation. A572 and A8549 were both still taxed at the start of Ulsterbus operations on 17 April 1967. Z7816 was not officially withdrawn until the end of 1965.

Parked on the former railway land at the rear of Oxford Street bus station is Leyland PD1 No Z908 (GZ 3264), new in 1946 and which carries a 53-seat, lowbridge body built by the NIRTB. This view was taken on 28 July 1965 and No Z908 survived in traffic to the end of 1966, the last of the batch of five to so do. Although it was extant on 17 April 1967, it was not taken into Ulsterbus stock.

In 1964, the Authority purchased 49 Bedford SB5s, which it bodied itself on Metal Sections frames. Some seated 40, but others, such as No T51 illustrated, had 51 seats, in 3+2 configuration, primarily for the carriage of schoolchildren. All of the 51-seaters had that capacity reduced to 49 by 1966 and all passed to Ulsterbus on 17 April 1967. The livery carried by No T51 is the eau-de-nil scheme also worn by the Leyland PD3s built between 1960 and 1963.

With the East Bridge Street bridge across the Belfast Central Railway in the background, Leyland PS1 No B8631 (GZ 7699), new in 1948 and A667 (GZ 6147), new in 1947, are parked up at the rear of Oxford Street on 28 July 1965. No A667 survived in traffic until the end of 1966, B8631 being withdrawn in October 1965. No A667 was another of those vehicles extant at 17 April 1967, but not taken into Ulsterbus stock.

The first order for new vehicles for Ulsterbus included a batch of 70 Bedford VAM5s with bodywork by Duple (Northern), though No 9208 carried a Willowbrook body. No 9206 (1206 TZ), renumbered with the rest of the batch to the 12XX series in 1969, is seen at the bus station in Kerr Street, Portrush, on 8 July 1967, when it was just a few months old. The livery was later altered to include a band of ivory on the mid-panels.

Still wearing the Ulster Transport Authority eau-de-nil livery and showing no sign of its Ulsterbus ownership, apart from the legal address details probably, AEC Reliance No 287 (6287 FZ) was photographed parked next to the old Great Northern Railway station in Foyle Road, Derry, on 8 July 1967. No 287, new in 1964, carries a UTA body built on Metal Sections frames and was part of a batch built for use on city services in Londonderry, though judging by the route number it had escaped on to the country route to Dungiven. The city AECs differed from similar Authority Reliances by having the emergency door in the rear and being lower-geared for climbing the many hills in the city.

In 1966, the UTA purchased from Edinburgh Corporation Transport 48 Weymann-bodied Leyland PSUC1/13 Tiger Cubs, which were numbered 9301–50; there was no No 9309 nor 9322. No 9338 (SWS 38), ex Edinburgh Corporation 38, obviously an early recipient of Ulsterbus Riviera Blue and Trader Ivory is seen parked at Foyle Road, Derry on 8 July 1967. Note the large italicised Roman fleetname applied to these early repaints. This batch of vehicles was renumbered 1001–50 in January 1969.

The first Leyland Tiger Cub to see service with the Authority was a Saro-bodied demonstrator, which arrived from Leyland Motors in 1954. This led to an order for 60 PSUC1/5T models, with in-house B43F bodies, Nos 302–61, which took up service in 1956/7. A further 59, with 41 coach seats and a slightly revised body, also entered service in 1957. Bus-seated No 310 was photographed by the Ulsterbus garage at Foyle Road, Londonderry on 8 July 1967.

The Authority also built the Alexander-style bodywork, seen earlier on AEC Reliance 287, on Albion Aberdonian and Leyland Tiger Cub chassis. Indeed, the Albions were the first so fitted. Here, in the very early days of Ulsterbus, and still in full Ulster Transport Authority livery, complete with crests, is No 71 (1071 XI) at Harbour Square, Londonderry, on 9 July 1967. No /1 was new in 1960.

On 9 July 1967, three Leyland PD3/4s – Nos 903 (903 AZ), 852 (8852 AZ) and 904 (904 AZ) – are seen at Custom House Street, Derry. No 852 was new in 1961, Nos 903/4 in 1960. The latter pair were fitted with power-steering for use on the then busy city service to the housing estate at Creggan, on the city side. Services to the Waterside area of the city passed through the Shipquay Gate and couldn't be operated with double-deckers.

In 1966, the Ulster Transport Authority acquired 15 Alexander-bodied Leyland Leopard L1s, new in 1960, from the Western Scottish Motor Traction Company of Kilmarnock, where they had been numbered JL1604–18 (OCS 726–40) and used on the overnight service between Glasgow and London. They ran, initially, in Western's black and white coach livery, complete with 30 luxurious, Chapman reclining seats and retaining the toilets. All were later re-seated with between 36 and 38 seats. All passed to Ulsterbus on 17 April 1967. Ulsterbus No 533, ex WSMT JL1611, was photographed on the Falls Road on 11 July 1967 when on service 104 to Lisburn via Derriaghy.

Our final Ulster Transport Authority/Ulsterbus view was taken near Bellevue, on Antrim Road, Belfast, on 20 July 1967, just three months into Ulsterbus operation. No 361 (UZ 361), still in the Authority's two shades of green and cream livery, is a Leyland Tiger Cub PSUC1/5T new in 1957 with bodywork built in-house by the Authority. One of Managing Director Werner Heubeck's early objectives was an increase in one-man-operation, to reduce costs and improve profitability, and No 361 has been fitted with a motor for the driver's Setright ticket machine.